AF444321

Dedication

This Children's Book is dedicated to my Parents who is the driving force behind everything I do in life. I miss them both a great deal.

Once upon a time, in a small city, there lived a little girl named Olivia. Olivia Loved Basketball. Every Saturday, she would sit on the blenchers, eyes wide, as she watched the local team play

The Sound of the ball bouncing, the swoosh of the net, and the cheers from the crowd filled her with excitement. Olivia dreamed of being a basketball star.

One sunny afternoon, Olivia decided it was time to start practicing. She grabbed her a small basketball and headed to the park.

As she dribbled, the ball felt heavy in her tiny hands, but she was determined.

She practiced shooting, running, and even trying to pass the ball to herself.

At First, it was tough. Other kids were taller and more skilled. Sometimes, Olivia felt like giving up. "Maybe I'll never be good enough she sighed", sitting on the bench

But Oliva remembered the spark of excitement she felt while watching the games.

With renewed determination, she stood up and
continued to practice. She focused on her
dribbling, her shots, and her footwork. Everyday,
she spent hours at the park, and slowly, she
began to improve.

One day, while practicing, Olivia noticed a group of kids playing a game, they were laughing, and having fun, but she felt a little shy. Taking a deep breath, she approached them. "Can I join; she asked.

The kids looked at her, then smiled. "of course.
We can use another player! "Olivia felt a rush of
joy as she ran unto the court. It was the best
decision she ever made.

As they played, Olivia learned the importance of teamwork, she passed the ball to her new friends and cheered them on. They help her improve her skills and, together, they became a strong team.

They practice drills, shared tips, and celebrated
each other's successes.

The day of the big championship game arrived. Olivia felt nervous as she stood in the locker room with her teammates. Olivia said to one of her teammates, "what if I mess up? She thought, biting her lips.
But her teammate Lushanna smiled and said, "just remember, we're all in this together. You're worked hard, and we believe in you.

As the game began, the crowd roared. Olivia played her heart out, running, passing, and shooting. She felt the adrenaline rush through her body, but when it was time for the final shot, she froze.

The score was tied, and Olivia took a deep breath, she remembered all those hours of practicing, her friends cheering her on, and her own love for the game.

With newfound confidence, she focused on the hoop and released the ball.

Swoosh! The ball went through the net and the crowd erupted in cheers. Olivia's teammates lifted her into the air, celebrating their victory.

Later, as they gathered around to celebrate, Olivia realized, something important. Winning was fantastic, but what mattered most were friendships she had made and the joy of playing together.

From that day on, Olivia Continued to practice and play, not just to become a star but to enjoy every moment on and off the court.

THE
END